# EXPLORING SPACE

BY ALLAN MOREY

BELLWETHER MEDIA · MINNEAPOLIS, MN

**Torque** brims with excitement
perfect for thrill-seekers of all kinds.
Discover daring survival skills, explore
uncharted worlds, and marvel at mighty
engines and extreme sports. In *Torque* books,
anything can happen. Are you ready?

This edition first published in 2023 by Bellwether Media, Inc.

No part of this publication may be reproduced in whole or in part without
written permission of the publisher. For information regarding permission,
write to Bellwether Media, Inc., Attention: Permissions Department,
6012 Blue Circle Drive, Minnetonka, MN 55343.

Library of Congress Cataloging-in-Publication Data

LC record for Exploring Space available at: https://lccn.loc.gov/2022012982

Text copyright © 2023 by Bellwether Media, Inc. TORQUE and associated
logos are trademarks and/or registered trademarks of Bellwether Media, Inc.

Editor: Kieran Downs     Designer: Josh Brink

Printed in the United States of America, North Mankato, MN.

# TABLE OF CONTENTS

# SPACE WALK

An **airlock** opens on the **International Space Station** (ISS). An **astronaut** floats out. A **tether** hooks her to the station. It is all that keeps her from drifting off into space.

INTERNATIONAL SPACE STATION

TETHER

EARTH

Below her, Earth comes into view. It is a bright blue ball of light against the blackness. Space holds many incredible sights!

# SPACE

The **vacuum** of space begins 62 miles (100 kilometers) above sea level. There is no air to breathe. Temperatures get very hot or incredibly cold.

SPUTNIK 1

YURI GAGARIN

Space exploration began in 1957 when Russia launched Sputnik 1. It was the first **artificial** object to **orbit** Earth. In 1961, Yuri Gagarin became the first person to reach outer space.

Soon, people set their sights on the moon. At about 238,855 miles (384,400 kilometers) away, it is the closest **celestial** body to Earth. In 1969, Apollo 11 became the first **mission** to reach the moon.

In 1998, construction started on the ISS. It was built in space. The first crew members began living there two years later!

APOLLO 11

ISS

# NOTABLE EXPLORER

**NAME:** KATHRYN SULLIVAN

**BORN:** OCTOBER 3, 1951

**JOURNEY:** IN 1984, WENT TO SPACE ABOARD THE SPACE SHUTTLE *CHALLENGER* AND PERFORMED A SPACE WALK

**RESULTS:** BECAME THE FIRST AMERICAN WOMAN TO PERFORM A SPACE WALK

Scientists travel to space to study it. They study what space does to living things. They hope to learn how people can survive long journeys through space. They also learn more about planets and stars.

People also travel to space as **tourists**. Flights take them on short trips to space.

## KÁRMÁN LINE

THE KÁRMÁN LINE IS AN IMAGINARY LINE. IT MARKS WHERE SPACE STARTS. IT IS NAMED AFTER SCIENTIST THEODORE VON KÁRMÁN.

# KÁRMÁN LINE

EARTH

SPACE

62 MILES
(100 KILOMETERS)

KÁRMÁN LINE =

# PLANNING AND PREPARATION

Astronauts must be trained. First, they train to be scientists or pilots. Then, they go through two years of astronaut training. They learn about being weightless in space. They learn medical and survival skills.

PILOT TRAINING

Astronauts do physical training, too.
They exercise regularly. They train their
bodies to get used to being weightless.

Before launch, astronauts go through a pre-flight checklist. They check all the equipment. They make sure safety systems work. They fill their food and water supplies for the journey. They gather tools for working in space.

They also watch the weather. Launches can only happen when conditions are right. When it is safe, the rocket takes off!

## EXERCISE

THE LACK OF GRAVITY IN OUTER SPACE WEAKENS BONES AND MUSCLES. ASTRONAUTS EXERCISE DURING MISSIONS TO KEEP THEIR BODIES HEALTHY.

# PLANNING YOUR JOURNEY

**TRAIN TO BE A SCIENTIST OR PILOT**

**TRAIN TO BE WEIGHTLESS**

**EXERCISE REGULARLY**

**DO PRE-LAUNCH CHECKS**

# ON THE JOURNEY

Journeys into outer space start at blastoff. Rockets must go fast enough to escape Earth's **gravity**. They lift into space at speeds of up to 25,000 miles (40,234 kilometers) per hour.

Once in outer space, the spacecraft's heaters keep astronauts warm. **Oxygen** tanks provide the air they need to breathe.

# WHAT HAPPENS IN SPACE WITHOUT A SUIT?

**NO AIR TO BREATHE**

**PASS OUT IN ABOUT 15 SECONDS**

**BODY EXPANDS TO TWICE ITS NORMAL SIZE**

**BODY SLOWLY FREEZES**

# ASTRONAUT'S ROOM

Storage aboard a spacecraft is very limited. Astronauts get little room to themselves.

Food is often **dehydrated**. It is stored in small packages. Water is added when it is time to eat! Astronauts drink from pouches through straws. This keeps water droplets from floating around and harming equipment.

DEHYDRATED FOOD

People continue to journey into space. Space tourism is growing. In 2021, the SpaceX program first launched tourists into space. Soon, more people will be able to explore space!

SPACEX LAUNCH

Astronauts continue to study outer space.
They make new scientific discoveries.
There is still much to explore in space!

# GLOSSARY

**airlock**—a chamber between two airtight doors that lets people enter and exit a space station

**artificial**—made by people

**astronaut**—a person who travels beyond Earth's atmosphere

**celestial**—having to do with objects in outer space; moons and planets are celestial bodies.

**dehydrated**—having water removed

**gravity**—the force that pulls objects towards other objects

**International Space Station**—a place for astronauts from all over the world to work in outer space

**mission**—a task that a person or group is ordered to do

**orbit**—to move around something in a circular path

**oxygen**—a gas needed to breathe

**tether**—a line or rope

**tourists**—people who travel to visit a place

**vacuum**—a place without matter

# TO LEARN MORE

## AT THE LIBRARY

Calkhoven, Laurie. *Human Missions to Outer Space*. New York, N.Y.: Children's Press, 2022.

Rector, Rebecca Kraft. *The International Space Station*. New York, N.Y.: Children's Press, 2022.

Yomtov, Nel. *Journeying to New Worlds*. North Mankato, Minn.: Capstone Press, 2023.

## ON THE WEB

# FACTSURFER

Factsurfer.com gives you a safe, fun way to find more information.

1. Go to www.factsurfer.com

2. Enter "exploring space" into the search box and click 🔍.

3. Select your book cover to see a list of related content.

# INDEX

The images in this book are reproduced through the courtesy of: Vadim Sadovski, cover (hero); Marc Ward, cover (ISS); Johan Swanepoel, cover (Meteorites); Andrey Armyagov, cover (satelite); muratart, cover (background space), CIP, p. 23; LWM/NASA/LANDSAT/ Alamy, pp. 4-5; Geopix/ Alamy, p. 5; Antonio Gil. Alamy, pp. 6-7; NSSDC/ Wikimedia Commons, p. 7 (Sputnik); TASS/ Alamy, p. 9 (Yuri Gagarin); NASA/ Wikimedia Commons, pp. 8-9; NASA/ Handout/ Getty Images, p. 9; NASA Photo/ Alamy, pp. 9, 10-11; (Kathryn Sullivan); zuperia, p. 9 (shooting star); Dotted Yeti, p. 9 (astronaut); NASA/ superstock, pp. 12-13; Artsiom Petrushenka/ Alamy, p. 13; Stocktrek Images/ Alamy, pp. 14-15; NASA/ Alamy, p. 15; Ryan Fletcher, p. 15 (learn to pilot); dpa picture alliance/ Alamy, p. 15 (train to be weightless); Mangostar, p. 15 (exercise); NASA, pp. 15 (pre-launch check), 17, 18, 19; Zenobillis/ Alamy, p. 16; Leremy, p. 17 (icons); Sipa USA/ Alamy, p. 20; Andrey Armyagov/ Alamy, p. 21.